CONTENTS

WELCOME

Right Rev Dr Russell Barr

Moderator of the General Assembly of the Church of Scotland

It is a delight to introduce another great edition of *Learn*.

Learn provides an exciting opportunity for a range of readers to enjoy high quality authors from throughout the Church.

Learning is at the heart of the Christian life and faith – the Greek word for 'disciple' means 'learner' – and with its wonderful vision of a church and school in every parish, education and learning was at the heart of the Reformation and remains a vital part of the Church of Scotland's life.

Tomorrow's Calling is one of the most important initiatives in the Church of Scotland. The ministries of the Church are varied and over the years I have found the ministry of Word and Sacrament to be fulfilling, demanding, challenging and rewarding in equal measure. As a trainee minister I learned so much from my student placements with Murray Leishman (Royal Edinburgh Hospital), Jack Kellet (South Leith), Tom Cuthell (St Cuthbert's), and I will always be grateful to them and to Ronnie Blakey (Jedburgh linked with Ancrum linked with Edgerston) who supervised me during my probationary period. Since being ordained in 1979 I have had the opportunity to supervise many students at different stages in their training and, as much as I hope they learned something from me, I have always learned something from them.

Following the publication of the *Ministers of the Gospel* report in 2000, the Church made a commitment to reflective practice and on-going learning as key principles in the training and formation of ministers. *Learn: Tomorrow's Calling* introduces a great number of ideas and reflections on discerning a call to ministry. I hope you make time to enjoy the articles, quietly reflect on the beautiful prayers and apply some of these great truths from the Christian tradition to your journey of discernment.

An exciting journey lies ahead of you, one in which you will learn a great deal about God, about yourself, and about the community around you; so let me wish you inspiration and blessing on this part of the journey, and encourage you in the knowledge that in the Christian life we are always learning. ∎

TOMORROW'S CALLING

Neil Glover
Convener, Ministries Council

I've checked the television for tonight – there is a chat show, a long-running quiz show, there's a preview of *Eurovision*, someone is going on a railway journey and there is a documentary about canals. All of these could have appeared on our televisions in the 1960s and 1970s. But there is something from that era which doesn't appear these days. The television schedule for tonight does not have Church of Scotland ministers giving a lecture on the historic background to Paul's first letter to the Corinthians. I made sure – I've checked it twice!

But this is the kind of thing that used to happen. William Barclay, a lecturer at Glasgow University, used to give these 'spellbinding' lectures on the New Testament, and Scottish audiences were rapt (it was deemed an insult when channel controllers in England shunted these programmes into a late-night slot; Scottish audiences wanted their New Testament exegesis at prime-time).

If you were a Protestant in Scotland, then for the most part this meant dealing with the Kirk, and ministers were bedded into the parish – they would visit their 1,000 members, and perform funerals for many more. The memoir of one inner-city minister casually mentions an incident that occurred on a day when he had seven weddings. Seven weddings! That's more in one day than I conducted last year.

It is not just in comparison with the 1960s that the change is marked. In the last two years, the vast majority of non-Catholic funerals in our parish were conducted by humanist celebrants. Church statistician Peter Brierley reports that of all the British denominations, by far the steepest decline in numbers has been experienced by the Church of Scotland.

It sometimes feels as though we in the Church are deeply rooted in a vision of Scottish life that hit its high point in the 1950s and 1960s. Scotland was about working hard and doing the right thing, about looking out for your neighbours, and being deeply conscious of human life in poorer countries. The Church of Scotland excelled at these things, and the Scottish people responded – they sat on the Kirk's pews, baked for the coffee mornings, put money in the offering plates, and (in the majority of occasions) revered the Church's reverends.

Ours is not the only Church facing decline, and ministry is not the only profession coming to terms with a changing role in Scotland. But the intensity of these things seems particularly pronounced in the Church of Scotland. My own sense is that we are particularly good at being a Church that related to mid-twentieth-century Scotland – even when we were satirised (Rikki Fulton's I.M. Jolly was a national icon) or lambasted for our perceived social conservatism (Scotland would only be free when the last Church of Scotland minister was strangled by the last copy of the *Sunday Post*, claimed the historian Tom Nairn[1]). We were part of the conversation, what we said mattered to people: people joined the Church even if at times it felt that people weren't joining out of a passionate zeal for the gospel, and more because it was the right thing to do.

So in this changing Scotland, what is the point of the Church of Scotland? And why might God still be calling ministers to a country that doesn't seem to want them as much as it used to? Why might God be calling you to this Church in this time of change?

As ministers lead worship each week they proclaim the message all over Scotland (and beyond) that God is here

For me there are three big reasons.

First, in crisis and change we are much more aware of our need to rely on God. We have to look to God for new ways forward instead of relying on traditional and conventional solutions, or trying to shore up inflexible institutions. The writer Phylis Tickle said that every 500 years the people of God have to go through a major reinvention. She traces this through Abraham, Moses and the flight from Egypt, David, Exile to Babylon, Jesus and the birth of the Church, monasticism and Gregory the Great, the divide between East and West, the Reformation and now. Every 500 years the Church has to have a giant rummage sale – discover God in new places instead of idolising the past. And now it's our turn to be broken so that we might become something new.

It is part of the exciting calling of ministers to think and pray about how the Church might be new in this change of age.

Second, the Church of Scotland still does some things incredibly well, and one of these is 'place'. The Church is dedicated to place. In hundreds of Scottish communities, it is the Church which remains at the heart of communities. Particularly when so many Council and Government services are being cut, it becomes vital for the Church to remain. Some people may care less about the Church of Scotland, but they probably still care about their community. They care about the flourishing of their communities, they care about those who find themselves on the margins, they want the best for our young people. And so does the Church, which is why it is still there. Eugene Peterson has written that the gospel is local intelligence, locally applied – and the Church's job is to invest energy and zeal into a particular place, regarding whoever happens to be on the premises as the people of God.[2] We do local, we do place, and in Scotland there is still a big place for place. As ministers lead worship each week they proclaim the message all over Scotland (and beyond) that God is here, and that God loves this place and this people.

And finally, the Church is needed because people might not go to church but they still wrestle with the same questions about their worth and their values. People worry about the future, or about the mistakes that they have made in the past. They still sense that this world is not all there is, and that something or someone has to be out there. And the Church and its ministers are called to respond to this, to talk about a gospel which offers meaning and hope, which speaks to the deepest questions of our lives. People might not regard themselves as religious, but fundamentally people haven't changed. I am constantly struck by the numbers of folk showing up at our church for a number of different reasons: a baby has been born, or because someone they loved has passed away, or just because they felt something within them telling them to come along. I am always struck by how appreciative people are when I offer to pray with them, or how amazed they are when the stories of Jesus in the Gospels are brought alive for them.

The culture of Scotland might have changed, but deep down the people remain constant. And ministers are called to share and embody a message which speaks to Scotland's people as truthfully now as it has for hundreds of years. ∎

tomorrowscalling.org

[1] http://www.ft.com/cms/s/0/705fc32e-5a4c-11dc-9bcd-0000779fd2ac.html#axzz439yhnqMn [accessed 17/03/16]
[2] Eugene Peterson, *Under the Unpredictable Plant: An Exploration in Vocational Holiness* (Grand Rapids, Michigan: Wm Eerdmans Publishing Co., 1992), p.130

Hearing a Call

My Story: being called by God

Jonathan Fleming

Calling to ministry, for me, came in instalments. I remember, as a teenager, sitting in evening worship at a Scripture Union camp in Alltnacriche watching a black and white video depicting the crucifixion as the Gospel account was read over it. I sat with tears in my eyes, a weight on my heart and a feeling that I wanted to know Jesus more. I had a conversation with one of the camp leaders about my experience and I knew that I wanted to follow Christ.

A few years later I became a camp leader for Scripture Union in Ballater. It was there that my father asked me if I had thought about following in my grandfather's footsteps and becoming a minister. I was 17 at the time and suffice to say I concluded it was not for me.

I threw myself into university life, and church went on the back burner for a few years. To begin with I went to Christian Union on a few occasions but I didn't feel that it was 'for me'; however, faith was always there, if slightly in the background.

Church was to reappear in my life in an unexpected way. Years later my friend Karyn (and now wife) was asked to play the piano and organ at a local church in Blantyre. Knowing that I knew my way around a church service, she asked if I would come along. That Sunday Karyn and I attended St Andrew's Parish Church in Blantyre, where we were warmly welcomed. Five minutes later, having been asked if I could sing, I was in the choir! We went back most weeks even though I was still living in Milngavie.

I enjoyed attending the church and began to become part of the life and worship there. Singing then led to reading the Scriptures, writing and saying the prayers and even preaching a sermon! These were skills and gifts which I had not used since my school days, and suddenly I was using them regularly in worship and it all felt very natural.

A couple of years later the pieces all began to fall into place. The calling to ministry became much clearer in my heart and mind and I realised that these gifts and talents that I enjoyed were actually part of the vocation that God was drawing me into and that I was beginning to hear more clearly.

GOD SPEAKS IN MANY WAYS

Ruth Harvey

Place for Hope, www.placeforhope.org.uk

I found myself at a crossroads. All my life I had felt a sense of deep commitment, a 'call', to the path of Christian living. But this time it was different. There were difficult choices now in front of me, and I was desperately seeking guidance, wisdom, clarity. I was looking inside myself: was this deep commitment, this sense of 'call' leading me to a particular profession in the Church? I turned to God, in prayer and meditations: sometimes in passionate conversation, other times in silence. At the same time I was looking to trusted friends and family to be direct and honest with me. And I looked to the Church for guidance, a sign, a sense of what the options might be, and how they might see me fitting in. Nothing at college, it seemed, had prepared me for this dilemma. Although I had learned about 'vocation' and 'discernment' and 'call', now that I had to make a decision, I had to ground this learning in my heart.

I asked a good friend for advice; he had been my supervisor in my first job. He said bluntly: 'Ruth, whatever option you choose, God is ahead of you.'

I was comforted by these words. But I still had to make a decision!

How do we know when God is speaking to us? How do we hear a call from God? We talk of call within the language of vocation. With its root in the Latin *vocatio*, this means call or summons.

Richard Niebuhr, a theologian living and working in the United States in the early twentieth century, wrote about four kinds of calling:
1. the call to be a Christian
2. the secret, or inward call to a particular role
3. the outward, or providential call from the world
4. the ecclesial, or community call.[1]

The call to be a Christian: Niebuhr names this the call to discipleship of Jesus Christ.[2] This universal calling, affirmed in our baptism, is a gift from God, and all of us who choose to follow Jesus Christ can own it. This call affirms that whoever we are, whatever our life story, whatever we choose to do, we have been called by God as his beloved child (Matthew 9.12–13; Luke 14.23).

The call to a particular role: Niebuhr describes this as a 'secret' call – secret in the sense that this is the inner knowledge, hunch or feeling that we are being asked to follow a very particular path within the Church. This secret call is often associated with nudgings of the Spirit that lead a person to consider a specific vocation as a way of living out his or her call to ministry. For some the call comes as a life-transforming event (like a thunderbolt) while for others it comes slowly (like the gradual, secret growing of a coral reef) and even with great wrestling.

The call from the world: This 'outward call' is the very practical exercise of accepting our gifts and our skills, noticing when and where these are affirmed in the world, and receiving these affirmations as holy guidance. Niebuhr talks about recognising that we have 'the talents necessary for the exercise of the office and through the divine guidance of his life by all its circumstances'.[3] This emerges from considering our God-given gifts and talents as well as our life experiences. To discern this call requires an honest look at our own life, our skills and our gifts, and questioning as well as confirmation from the community of faith.

The call of the church community: A friend attended a Vocations Conference to be sure that he was being called to the ministry of Word and Sacrament. Throughout the day, listening to the input, spending time in quiet reflection, talking with those he knew in his church, he heard affirmed from many different voices in the church not only his ministry in school teaching, but also his prophetic ministry in the

> **" For some the call comes as a life-transforming event _(like a thunderbolt)_ while for others it comes slowly.**

church as a leader on a number of important campaigns and projects. His existing calling was affirmed by others in the church in a way that surprised and delighted him. Had he not been open to this call of the church, he would have missed a vital part of the vocation journey.

God speaks in many ways to us: through the Church, through our community of trusted friends, through our own gifts and talents honed over time, and through an inner sense of vocation. We may experience one or more of these calls simultaneously, or at different times in our life. How we stay alive to God, to these different voices, is a lifelong journey. Developing and nurturing regular disciplines can be helpful to 'hearing' our call. Some of these disciplines are:

Read

Richard Niebuhr, **The Purpose of the Church and its Ministry** (New York, London: Harpers, 1977)

Anne Long, **Listening** (London: Daybreak, 1990)

See also: Learn: Eldership (Edinburgh: Saint Andrew Press, 2014), p.12

Think

1. Which daily disciplines would enable you to be open to hearing God's call?

2. Have you had any experiences which suggested the presence of an 'inward' call to ministry?

3. Explore your own sense of the call of the community, or what Niebuhr calls the 'outward' call.

Act

Why not, alone or in a group, take time away on a retreat, or spend a portion of a day in silent prayer, listening to God?

- prayer, reflection on Scripture, shared times of worship
- open and honest sharing with friends about vocation and ministry
- ongoing learning and reflection about our own gifts and talents
- openness to the opportunities and invitations offered by our church community
- the ability to discern when to say 'yes' and when to say 'no'.

As a beloved child of God, we are each unique. Our calling to ministry, of whatever kind, will also be unique. I set out on the journey to ministry unsure about what *job* I would do. As it turned out, I have had a number of different jobs, but in each of them I have remained confident that 'God goes ahead of me.' And like the pilgrim posts that guide the traveller along the causeway which crosses the sands to Lindisfarne, while we can't always see the posts in the far distance, all we need to make the journey is sight of the very next post, and confidence that God is with us. ■

[1] See: Richard Niebuhr, *The Purpose of the Church and its Ministry* (New York, London: Harper's, 1977), p.64
[2] Niebuhr, *The Purpose of the Church and its Ministry* (New York, London: Harper's, 1977), p.64
[3] Niebuhr, *The Purpose of the Church and its Ministry*, p.64

Paul and Moses
everyone is different

Acts 9.1-19

Alison Jack
New College, University of Edinburgh

The story of Paul's conversion (Acts 9.1–19) has all the drama of a supernatural thriller. Enter Paul the rabbi, a man with a mission to seek out and crush the followers of Christ. He is not content just to remonstrate with those he happens to encounter in his everyday life. Rather, he goes out of his way to discover and confront those he believes are threatening all he holds dear. Quite possibly religious and political fear lies at the heart of his actions.

And then in the most public and dramatic way comes divine intervention. Lights flash from heaven. A voice is heard, not just by Paul but by his companions, too. And a question is posed to him: 'Why? ... Why are you persecuting me?' Paul, thrown to the ground by the force of the encounter, is totally surprised and perplexed, although he perhaps recognises that God is at work – 'Who are you, Lord?' he asks the voice; and the reply could not be clearer. This is the very person whose followers he has been pursuing, the Jesus he has, by extension, been seeking to destroy.

A final, horrifying surprise awaits Paul. When he rises to go, he is told to wait for further instruction, and realises he has been blinded. His spiritual blindness is represented in the most graphic manner. His physical and spiritual lack of sight/insight awaits the further revelation which a man sent by God will bring. When his calling is confirmed, he will truly 'see' again. His will be a calling to witness to those in darkness, to the Gentiles who have never heard God's message. And for that Paul needs the new vision of one who has had his whole life turned round by an encounter with Christ.

When his calling is confirmed, he will truly 'see' again.

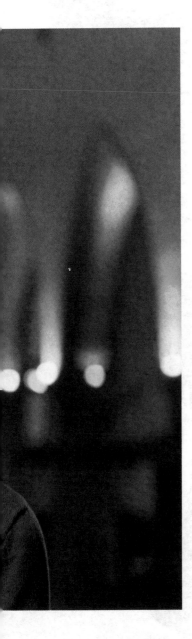

In contrast, Moses' calling seems to be a much less immediately persuasive experience (Exodus 3.1-4.17). There is drama: a bush on fire that does not burn up; and a voice from the bush which quickly identifies itself as coming from God. Moses knows what to do, and covers his face in the presence of the divine. But realising he is being addressed by God does not stop him from disagreeing with everything the voice tells him to do at every turn. 'Go and tell the king of Egypt to let my people go,' says the voice; 'I am nobody,' says Moses, 'Why should the king or the people for that matter believe me?' God reveals his name to Moses, and offers him two miraculous proofs – the staff that turns into the snake, and the healed hand. Still Moses equivocates. His next response is the decider, he thinks: 'I am no communicator, my speech is poor.' When God persists, finally Moses is honest, more or less admitting: 'I'm scared. I don't want to do it. Send someone else, anyone but me.' It has been many years since Moses was in a position of power at court: little wonder his confidence has been knocked. But God has an answer to that too, in the form of Aaron his brother, the smooth talker. Together they will form a powerful team. And Moses seems to realise he has played his last hand, and takes the first step towards a life-changing encounter with Pharaoh.

We may not hear the voice of God as directly or as dramatically as Moses or Paul did, but we may recognise something of our own experience in their stories. An experience which stops us in our tracks, which forces us to think again and maybe even turn our lives around. Or a completely different experience, of debate and struggle, of finding reasons to resist; an experience of fear and a sense of inadequacy in the face of what seems to be being asked of us. Paul and Moses are among the big characters of the Bible narrative, and the stories of their calling by God suit their large yet different literary personae. We too are treated as individuals by God when it comes to the way God leads, inspires and guides us. Like Moses and Paul, we may find that the voice of God speaking our name, whether it comes to us as a shout or a whisper, is difficult to ignore. ■

Read

Terry Biddington, **Risk-Shaped Discipleship: On Going Deeper into the Life of God** (San Jose, California: Resource Publications, 2010), pp.45–56

Anthony B. Robinson and Robert W. Wall, **Called to be Church: The Book of Acts for a New Day** (Grand Rapids: Eerdmans, 2006), pp.132–149

F. Scott Spencer, **Journeying through Acts: A Literary-Cultural Reading** (Peabody, Mass.: Hendrickson Publishers, 2004)

Think

1. Read a little more about the life of Paul in the book of Acts and in his letters. In what ways does God's interaction with him suit his character?

2. Read a little more about the life of Moses from the book of Exodus. Again, in what ways is it the same with Moses?

3. Compare these stories to other call stories in the Bible (such as the calling of Isaiah in Isaiah 6.1–7, or of Andrew and Peter in Matthew 4.18–20). Are there features in common? Or significant differences?

Act

Read both stories again, allowing the characters and the events to come alive in your imagination. Prayerfully consider if God is speaking to you through either or both.

A LIFE IN MINISTRY

All sorts of very different people are selected and trained
for ministry in the Church of Scotland.

Hear their stories at
www.tomorrowscalling.org/a-life-in-ministry

TOMORROW'S
CALLING

tomorrowscalling.org

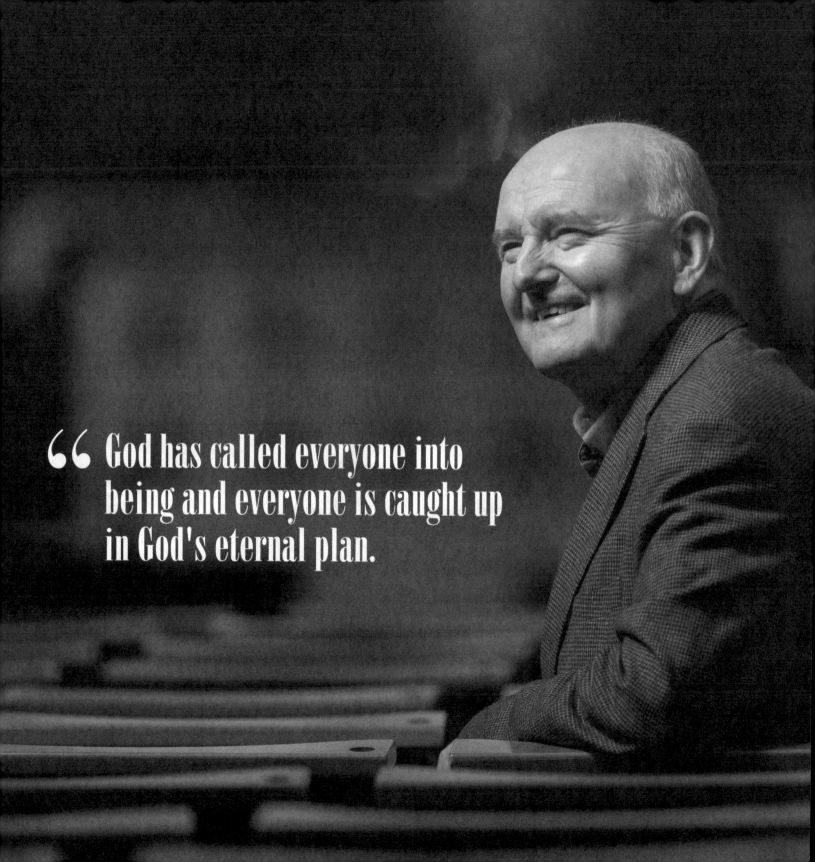

" God has called everyone into being and everyone is caught up in God's eternal plan.

STARTING THE JOURNEY

David Scott
Minister of Traprain

Quite by chance, David Esterly was taken by his fiancée to see the altarpiece in St James' Church, Piccadilly. It had been designed and made by the Dutch wood-carver, Grinling Gibbons. Although Esterly knew nothing of Gibbons, when he saw the delicate and detailed wood carvings, he was immediately absorbed in the beauty of it all.

He had a physical reaction to what he saw. It was like one of the wonders of the world. His steps slowed down. The palms of his hands were tingling. Everything around him went silent. It seemed as if he was 'at the still centre of the universe'.[1]

Responding to this experience, he decided to do some research on Gibbons and began to write about his wood-carvings. It seemed the most natural way for a student of English Literature to proceed. In order to deepen his understanding of the craftsman, he decided to buy a chisel and try his hand at carving.

Curiously, this was the beginning of a career which took him to the burnt-out shell of Hampton Court where he recreated one of Gibbons' masterpieces! The result was his beautiful memoire, 'The Lost Carving', in which he reveals how a hidden talent surfaced accidentally when he entered 'the still centre of the universe'. Perhaps this was more providential than accidental?

What was it that stirred within him? How did the carved wood generate such an extraordinary reaction? What was it that led him to write about Grinling Gibbons and then become his alter ego? Was this what we might call a vocation?

Notwithstanding the fact that this experience took place within a church and 'at the still centre of the universe', there is no mention of God in Esterly's understanding of what happened. One thing is sure. He came alive and found his true self, his destiny, even in the carving of lime-wood.

As well as the vocation to be a Christian and the vocation to be a minister, there is the vocation 'to be'. God has called everyone into being and everyone is caught up in God's eternal plan. The ministry of Jesus is famously summarised in the word 'salvation' which is all about healing and wholeness and God's plan to bring unity and peace to the whole creation.

Everyone has a part to play in this, as we see in the book of Esther. Esther is an orphan brought up by her cousin Mordecai. She wins a beauty competition and becomes queen, but the king doesn't know that she is a Jew, and when her people are put in danger, she is obliged to summon up all her courage and reveal her true identity to the king.

Mordecai realises Esther's vocation when he asks her the question, 'Who knows? Perhaps you have come to royal dignity for just such a time as this?' (Esther 4.14). It was remarkable that she was queen at such a time and was able to use her gifts to save her people.

Time has such a significant part to play in vocation and the fulfilment of God's plan. The Greek New Testament distinguishes between *chronos*, chronological time, and *kairos*, the time of opportunity. Esther had a choice whether to fulfil her vocation or not, whether to seize the opportunity or not. And so do we, for we are all called into being by God for such a time as this.

Through our baptism, our calling 'to be' is brought into the context of the Church and the opportunities we have to realise our true vocation. Peter uses two images to describe the members of the Church. The first is as living stones, which has behind it the description of Christ as the stone which the builders rejected: 'Like living stones, let yourselves be built into a spiritual house' (1 Peter 2.5). The first step in discerning our vocation is to let ourselves be built into this spiritual house: finding ourselves in the Church and being a part of the whole enables us to start discerning our gifts and how they may be used. We should take time to enjoy being a part of this and seeing what it means to be built together.

The second image that Peter uses is that of a holy priesthood (1 Peter 2.5). There is only one priest and that is Christ. But in our life together as the people of God, we participate in the priesthood of Christ by offering sacrifices of praise in our worship and love in our service. We are all called to be ministers of his grace.

For some, this vocation to be a minister of God's grace is focused on a ministry of Word and Sacrament, for others it may be the office of the eldership or the readership, or perhaps it may be a ministry of hospitality, of social work, of serving those on the margins of society or of an artist sharing in the creativity of God.

Whatever our calling, we are all part of God's creation and we all participate in the fulfilment of God's plan. Being alive, being responsive to others, being built into a spiritual house, and being part of the holy priesthood constitute our vocation to glorify God as we minister his grace and discover the exciting part which we can play 'at the still centre of the universe'. ∎

Read

David Esterly, **The Lost Carving** (London: Duckworth Overlook, 2013)

Graham Tomlin, **The Widening Circle** (London: SPCK, 2014)

Francis Dewar, **Called or Collared** (London: SPCK, 2000)

Think

1. Think about an experience which made you excited to be alive. To what extent did this experience open you up to God?

2. Look back over your life and pick out three experiences in which you seized an opportunity. What personal characteristics and gifts did these experiences illuminate?

3. Think about being part of the Church and what you find fulfilling. How might these things help you to discern what God is calling you to be?

Act

Read the story of Esther in the Bible. Ask yourself: what is it about today that might make me say, 'It is for this day that I have been born!'?

[1] David Esterly, *The Lost Carving* (London: Duckworth Overlook, 2013), p.44

LISTEN FOR MY NAME

Roddy Hamilton

When I was born
You named me Love:
love full of imagination;
shaped by compassion;
blessed with gifts I did not yet know
yet revealed in the world daily
through me being me.

When I was baptised
You named me Love
love born against the darkness
and towards the light
a gift within community
set free daily
through me being me.

As I live
you name me Love
love nurtured
in my questions and wonder
in my words and silence
unfolding faith daily
through me being me.

May I have eyes to see
and ears to hear
the deeper times
that hold the moments that make me think
that wrestle with the events that turn my head
that speak the words that call me anew

that I may make the time
to listen for my name
called each day
to be:

Love
Hope
Companion
Adventurer

in everything I do.

Amen

Discerning a Call

My Story: being called to ministry

Sheena Orr

A hotel room in Thornaby! That's where I began to realise that God really wanted my attention. I was doing some work for Church Action on Poverty – with people on the edge, which has always been my calling – but becoming increasingly aware that I should be loosening ties to my consultancy work. I would come back in the evening, sit there and burst into tears ... not because of the work but because of something I can't really describe. A 'pull' inside of me, like a rope attached to my stomach and pulling from behind the scenes – pulling, pulling, pulling. I spoke to my husband who could quite clearly see that 'something' was going on and we agreed that we would take it a step at a time. I had already been going away for retreat days at The Bield in Perthshire to pray and seek guidance and to talk to people about this 'pull' to ministry that I was feeling. And so in 2006 I went to a Church of Scotland Enquirers' Conference.

A jigsaw piece gave the clue to the way ahead. A box of jigsaw pieces was handed around in one of the early sessions at the Enquirers' Conference. I dipped my hand in without looking and pulled out an edge piece. This confirmed my sense that whatever I was being called to was not mainstream. I had the sense then, which continued throughout my formation, that I was being called to something different ... but to what I couldn't quite say. At first I found this alarming as so often we were asked to 'articulate our calling'. I felt mine was very difficult to articulate in terms of words and yet the feeling and spiritual affirmation was so sure. It was to be a year or so before I read the words of Oswald Chambers that articulated just what I felt: 'The call of God is like the call of the sea — no one hears it except the person who has the nature of the sea in him. What God calls us to cannot be definitely stated, because His call is simply to be His friend to accomplish His own purposes.'[1]

I heard the call, a compelling pull to ordained ministry, all the while having a growing sense that I would be a round peg in a square hole. God sometimes calls round pegs!

[1] http://utmost.org/the-bewildering-call-of-god/ [accessed 20/09/15]

CALLING IN THE CHURCH OF SCOTLAND

Frances Henderson
Minister of Hoddom, Kirtle-Eaglesfield & Middlebie Church

> Christians are not merely the recipients of God's salvation; they are also part of God's plan for salvation.

In the Communion liturgy in the Church of Scotland, just after the Narrative of the Institution, a version is used of the following words: 'I take these elements of bread and wine, to be set apart from all common uses to this holy use and mystery.'[1]

This sentence, about 'setting apart', is an important concept when thinking about calling in the Reformed tradition. The bread and wine are ordinary things, everyday food and nothing exceptional in themselves. Nor does anything happen to them when they are used in Communion – they remain ordinary bread and wine. But this particular bread and wine have been 'set apart' by us for a particular holy purpose. And God can use this ordinary stuff to do something miraculous: to make Jesus present to us when we take the bread and wine in faith.

Something very similar happens when a person is ordained in the Church of Scotland, whether as an elder, a minister, or a deacon. No grand claims are made about that person being changed in any way: they remain 'ordinary stuff', no better or worse than anyone else. And yet that ordinary stuff has now been 'set apart' for a particular holy purpose. God can do something miraculous through them, for the Church is the Body of Christ, and so those who have been set apart become one of the means by which Jesus can become present to the world.

This is a big claim to make, and some people are nervous of making it. And that is understandable: what is meant to be a truly humbling doctrine, that God can use even sinners like you and me for a holy purpose, can easily lead to an over-inflated sense of self-importance among the ordained. Some balance can be regained by remembering that the ordained are not alone in being set apart. In the Reformed tradition, we believe that every single Christian is called and set apart for just such a holy purpose. So a call to ordained service must take its place within the multitude of callings that are shared among the whole people of God.

Central to the Reformed tradition from the very start has been the doctrine of election. This doctrine is based particularly upon the teachings of the apostle Paul in Romans 8-11, although Jesus also speaks of 'the elect'' (Matthew 24.24, 31; Mark 13.20, 27), as does Peter in his second letter (2 Peter 1.10). 'Election' means simply 'a choice', and here it refers to God's choice. In the Old Testament literature 'the Elect' refers to the people of Israel – God's chosen ones. Then, in the New Testament, 'the Elect' expands to include Christians who, like the people of Israel, have been chosen and called and set apart from all other peoples to be part of God's plan of salvation.

The doctrine of election in the Reformed tradition has been controversial since the beginning. The Geneva Reformer John Calvin wrestled with the problem of what happens to those who are not elect – has God explicitly rejected them and consigned them to hell? It would be an uncomfortable thought if God were to play favourites in this way, especially since there is nothing we can do about it. And in his classic novel, *The Private Memoirs and Confessions of a Justified Sinner* (1824), James Hogg shows how distorted the doctrine can become, as his protagonist, who believes he is one of the elect, commits worse and worse sins, with (he thinks) no consequences, so confident is he that his salvation is assured.

Again, a doctrine which is supposed to be humbling – that God has chosen us, not because we are good or holy, but out of sheer love and grace in divine freedom – can easily be given the wrong emphasis. The doctrine of election does not tell us what happens to non-Christians. It is not designed to do that. It simply tells us that Christians have been set apart. Like the bread and the wine, they have been set apart for a holy purpose, to witness to Jesus Christ in the world. Christians are not merely the recipients of God's salvation; they are also part of God's plan for salvation. So it is not enough to believe that Christians have been set apart *from* the world. The important point is that they have been set apart *for* the world.

It is worth stating again: Christians have been called *out* of the world so that they might be for the world. The twentieth-century Reformed theologian Karl Barth emphasised how the first object of election is Jesus Christ himself, as God chose to be for humanity in him. As his disciples, those who follow Jesus are also called to be for the world: to live out the meaning of the incarnation in which God blessed the world with his own presence. This calling will take us on a path of service and sacrifice for the sake of the world, as we take up our cross to follow Jesus Christ.

In other words, every single Christian has been set apart for a holy purpose of witness and service in and to the world. The early Reformers rejected the idea that ordinary Christians

who worked at ordinary jobs were somehow spiritually inferior to those who lived a religious life in a monastery or convent or who were secular priests. Both Calvin and Martin Luther believed that the true Christian calling was into the world, and not out of the world.

The idea of the 'priesthood of all believers' (see 1 Peter 2.5-9) in this connection means that all Christians share in the priesthood of Christ, because in Jesus, the great High Priest, we too have been chosen and sent, not to condemn the world but to pray for and serve the world, witnessing in the power of the Spirit to the good news in Jesus Christ.

This means that we have been sent to work in a variety of professions and, in so doing, we can share in the priestly work of Christ in the world. This applies to every single occupation to which Christians might find themselves called. In short, work outside the Church can be no less a calling than work in the Church. Those who work outside the Church are called to express their love for God and for neighbour; they are called to demonstrate their care for, and stewardship of, the world; and they are called to channel our human inventiveness in productive and disciplined directions. The ordinary stuff of life, when dedicated to God's glory, can serve a holy purpose.

Work can also be praise. This means that, for Christians, the world cannot easily be divided into 'sacred' and 'secular'. God calls every Christian to a particular service in the world, and it is for each one of us to discern through prayer and devotion how we might best serve God. For some, this may mean a calling to full-time ministry in the Church. For others, it may mean continuing as they are, serving God in their workplace or in their community, for such work can be holy too as it is dedicated to the glory of God in praise and prayer. And for all of us, it is important to maintain a continual, prayerful openness to God calling us in a new direction. ∎

> **" The ordinary stuff of life, when dedicated to God's glory, can serve a holy purpose.**

Read

Alastair McGrath, **Calvin and the Christian Calling, in First Things 94** (1999), pp.31-35

www.firstthings.com/article/1999/06/calvin-and-the-christian-calling

George Herbert, **The Elixir (poem), in The English Poems of George Herbert** (London: J. M. Dent & Sons, 1974), p.188

Donald K. McKim, **'The 'Call' in Reformed Tradition'**, in Donald K. McKim ed., **Major Themes in the Reformed Tradition** (Eugene, Oregon: Wipf & Stock Publishers, 1998), pp.335-343

Think

1. Think about the different kinds of work you do in the world. Where can you see holiness in your work?

2. The doctrine of election follows Scripture in saying that Christians have been chosen by God. How do you feel about being chosen specially by God? What do you think you have been chosen for?

3. There is a danger in church life that we value some callings above others. How can we better affirm the holiness of all callings?

Act

Ask different people to share with the congregation or home group something of what the work they have done in their lives has involved. Where have they seen God in their work?

Samuel and Eli
seeking guidance

1 Samuel 3.1-9

Alison Jack
New College, University of Edinburgh

Samuel is dedicated to God in more ways than one. His mother gives thanks for the miracle of his birth, the answer to her prayers, by dedicating him to the service of Eli in the temple. At several points in the preceding story, Samuel's dedication to Eli and to the people is commented upon favourably – he has embraced the life to which his parents entrusted him. And yet, we are told, he 'did not yet know the Lord'. Perhaps this is not surprising, because apparently words and visions from the Lord were rare at this time – perhaps because there was corruption at the heart of Eli's family which he seemed unwilling or unable to sort out. So, Samuel is dedicated, but still in the dark. Nevertheless, his ears and eyes are open, while Eli's are growing dim.

God's call to Samuel comes in the form of his name. It is personal and direct. But apparently God's voice sounds so much like Eli's voice that Samuel assumes it is his human master who is calling him from the inner part of the temple. On being repeatedly wakened by Samuel, at first Eli too is perplexed. But his years of experience and faithful presence in the temple finally suggest to him that the mystery voice may have a divine origin. He offers Samuel a suitable response: 'Speak, Lord, for your servant is listening.' Perhaps Samuel doesn't quite believe what Eli is telling him, that God himself is addressing him in the night, because when he responds to the next calling of his name, he misses out the address 'Lord'. He is keeping his options open. But Eli is proved right, and Samuel receives a shocking and detailed explanation of what is to happen next in the temple complex.

However dedicated we are to the workings of the Church, however long or short a time we have spent around Christian people and ideas, we may all have blind spots or places we aren't willing to go when it comes to hearing the calling of God for us. The story of Samuel's call suggests that guidance may come from the most unlikely, as well as from the most obvious, places. The obvious: those more experienced in the faith than we are; people in authority in the Church used to handling theological concepts. The less obvious: those who struggle to get things right in the service of the Lord; those who make

...God's call is not a one-off event, which you miss at your peril.

mistakes and are unsure about the way ahead for themselves. The complex character of Eli was all of these. He was flawed, but Samuel knew and trusted him.

Perhaps the more we know and trust someone, the more likely we are to take their advice seriously, even if we are aware of the difficulties they face in their own lives. God does not leave himself without witnesses in the world, and we may find that those closest to us have a role to play in guiding us towards hearing God's call and understanding what it means for us. Everyone and everything Samuel needed to respond to God's call was at hand, the legacy of the dedication of his parents and his own willingness to listen. He didn't need to disappear on retreat or seek out the advice of expert strangers – although these tactics might sometimes be appropriate, of course!

The story also reassures us that God's call is not a one-off event, which you miss at your peril. Instead, it speaks of God's patience in the face of Samuel's uncertain jumping to all the wrong conclusions. Samuel's experience takes place in the space of a night, but the timing of events is less important than the persistence of God. Three times God tries to make contact with Samuel, willing him to find the advice which will enable him to understand. Eli's confidence that God will not give up on Samuel is one of his gifts to the boy and to us as readers. All Samuel has to do is return to the place where he has already encountered the voice. Finding that place, whether it is a physical or a mental or spiritual space, and returning to it having sought the advice of those we trust, may be a way to discern the call that we have heard, the call that we cannot quite believe had a divine origin and was directed at us. ∎

Read

Mary J. Evans, **The Message of Samuel** (Leicester: IVP, 2004)

David F. Payne, **I & II Samuel: The Daily Study Bible Series** (Louisville: WJK, 1982)

Jonathan Draper, **To Love and Serve: Being the Body of Christ in a Time of Change** (London: SPCK, 2003)

Think

1. Samuel is still a boy at the time of this encounter with God's voice. Consider in what ways that may have had an impact upon hearing and understanding God's call.

2. Are there ways in which the Christian community can offer support, advice and encouragement to those who hear God's call but resist it, or to those who believe they hear a call, while others are not so sure?

3. Hearing a call may have implications, not always positive, for those closest to the person being called. What support should they be given?

Act

If you have begun to wonder if God is calling you in a specific way, share your thoughts with someone you trust, and be ready to hear their advice.

CALLING WITHIN THE COMMUNITY

David McNeish
Minister of Birsay, Harray & Sandwick

When God calls, he calls in community. If there is no community, there is no calling. You may believe you are the answer to every problem in the church, but if no one else agrees then you risk becoming yet another problem. It is with and through other people that we discover our calling, and it is with and through other people that we can live out that calling. This is what makes serving God so satisfying, and so terrifying. Calling is a community endeavour.

Everyone who desires to serve God is called from a community, called in a community and called to a community. We'll consider each of these in turn.

Called from a community

Where you come from matters. It doesn't define you, but it does shape you. Our understanding of community starts with our experience of it, both positive and negative. Moses was an Israelite who grew up in a privileged Egyptian household, while Jesus was a provincial carpenter's son who astonished and enraged the establishment. We all have a back story and it matters. And it is out of this context that we are called. God speaks in language we can understand and God can and does speak through people around us – people who can help identify our gifts, notice our skills and encourage us in our calling.

When I was considering ministry I met up with a retired minister and admitted I was worried I was only pursuing ministry because I was trying to be Jesus. Quick as a flash he said 'Och, every minister thinks they're the Messiah, it's what you do about it that counts!'

Called in a community

It is easier to work alone. There are fewer arguments, plus the Christmas night out is cheaper! But we are called to serve in a community. One paradox is that we have something unique to contribute and yet we are not indispensable. It is worth taking the time to appreciate your own strengths and weaknesses and to look at who around you can help contribute what it is you lack. No one is the full package, despite what the vacancy adverts might say. At the same time, be careful not to pigeon-hole yourself or other people. Observe others and learn from them and you'll find yourself gaining skills and insights you didn't think you could have. The more you can appreciate what others contribute, the more you can encourage them in it, and encouragement is a vital part of ministry, whatever kind of ministry you are involved in.

I saw this in practice as a member of a high school chaplaincy team where a pupil died tragically in an accident. The strengths and diversity of that team were tested beyond what any of us thought we were capable of. And through it some extraordinary

**66 Calling is a
community
endeavour**

Read

John Allen, **Rabble Rouser for Peace: The Authorised Biography of Desmond Tutu** (London: Rider Books, 2006)

Ron Ferguson, **Chasing the Wild Goose: The Story of the Iona Community** (Glasgow: Wild Goose Publications, 1998)

Eugene Peterson, **Under the Unpredictable Plant: An Exploration in Vocational Holiness** (Grand Rapids: Eerdmans, 1992)

Stanley Hauerwas, **Hannah's Child: A Theologian's Memoir** (Grand Rapids: Eerdmans, 2012)

things happened, making use of the very different talents and abilities in the team. Yet we were still most united in our heartfelt wish that it hadn't happened at all.

Called to a community

The likelihood is that at some stage you will move location. Whether because of the kind of ministry you are drawn towards, or because of other circumstances, you can find yourself in a different community. And every community is different. Often this is when you discover that the assumptions you have made about the community are wrong, because they are not shared in the community you join – or, more accurately, the communities. The church community, the pub community, the school community, the farming community, the business community – each one overlaps with the others but is also different. The challenge is not getting stuck in any one but being able to serve the whole community as much as it is possible for any one person to do. Often, the joy of ministry is seeing connections being made – connections between God and people, and between different people, blurring boundaries, challenging assumptions and encouraging people to risk being vulnerable with others and with God. Most ministry in most communities is under the radar – it will never make the news; it is unseen and, sometimes, unappreciated. But it is so worthwhile.

I never imagined when I entered ministry that I would end up serving in the West Mainland of Orkney. I grew up in Cumbernauld and Milngavie and spent all my adult life in and around Edinburgh. I know nothing about farming. Yet it is where my family and I have been called and it is a surprisingly good fit. I bring pastoral skills to a pastoral community and sometimes being an outsider is exactly what is needed. All forms of ministry can be lonely at points – you are at once an integral part of a community and outside of it. Learning to live with this paradox takes time and wisdom. Yet you are privileged to walk with people through the very best and very worst of times. I've noticed how the landscape changes because of these experiences. Houses begin to have stories attached, as do gravestones. Memories of encounters change how you see and what you see around you. The more I minister, the more I agree with Gerard Manley Hopkins that 'the world is charged with the grandeur of God'. God is at work in every community. The delightful thing is being allowed to participate. ■

Think

1. Think about where you are from – in what ways has it shaped you and how might it affect the way you serve others, both positively and negatively?

2. Think about aspects of ministry that are not your strength – what kind of people and gifts do you need around you to complement what you can offer?

3. Think about people who are missing from your community - how can you make connections with these groups and individuals?

Act

Take some time to find out first-hand about a section of the community you know nothing about, for example visit a prison, a youth club, a dance group. Ask questions which broaden your understanding and challenge your assumptions.

DISCERNING TOGETHER

Lynn McChlery
Associate Minister of Cambuslang: Flemington Hallside

'So you want to be a minister?' the careers adviser asked. 'Was that your own idea, or have you just been badly advised?' Many of us wondering if we were being called secretly feel the same. Is it just a mad idea? Am I making it up? How can I be sure that it's not just my own idea, or even someone else's advice? How do I know that it is God's idea for my life?

There is no easy shortcut in discernment. Private prayer, listening to God and inner conviction are vitally important, alongside talking with others. Thankfully, nobody has to do it alone: we are in this together.

In the book of Acts (chapters 10-15) we read a fascinating story of how this worked in the early church: Cornelius' call to faith is relayed to Peter; discussed by the group of believers; prayed over and argued about; tested by Scripture; re-told and distilled until its significance is clear; then formally affirmed by a Church Council. And I thought our processes were long and complicated! Discernment has consistently been an activity of the church together: it is 'our calling' rather than simply 'my calling'.

If God is speaking to you about a particular form of service in the Church, it makes sense that God will be prompting other people too, and eventually the Church will come to recognise that together. The Church of Scotland has a recognised process for discernment, and people at every stage who will listen, support, and test with you to find what is your unique vocation.

What's the process? After attending a Vocations Conference, the next step is to start a formal Period of Discernment with a minister who is also a trained Mentor. It usually would not be in your own congregation. That helps you to see another church, and another minister, at close range – and to keep your home church as 'home'! You will agree with your Mentor to spend some hours each week shadowing him/her in order to see different aspects of parish ministry. You will also meet a Presbytery Representative, another minister to be a conversation partner and to offer different experiences and perspectives.

During this time of discernment you have the opportunity to try things out and find what is right for you. It is a time to find what resonates with your gifts and your sense of yourself, and discover where you sense fulfilment in God's calling. Alongside the practical, a vital part of the discernment period is growing in prayer, reading about God's call, writing your insights in a journal, and reflecting with your Mentor the different ways in which God's call is becoming clear to you .

Some people realise through this period that ministry of Word and Sacrament is not for them – they are called to follow Jesus and build God's kingdom in a different way. That is fine, and you can withdraw from the process at any time. It's all about finding what is right for you.

After a suitable period, usually around six months, there will be a Local Review. You will meet formally with your Mentor, Presbytery Representative and a National Assessor to discuss your experiences so far, and they will decide whether you are ready to go forward to a National Assessment Conference. If you are, you will go to a residential conference to be assessed by three Assessors (one of them a psychologist). You will be in a group of about four other people in discernment, which is a great opportunity to meet others on a similar journey. You will have a chance to share your story so far in a supportive environment, with people who are trained to listen sympathetically and weigh what you say. References from your own church and reports from your Discernment Period are all taken into account, and the Assessors together decide whether the Church of Scotland affirms your call, at this time, to ministry of Word and Sacrament.

It is a testing process, as you would expect of such a serious matter, but fundamentally it is about listening for God together. Sometimes there is disappointment if the Church of Scotland decides that you are better suited to another form of ministry, or that you may be called but not yet. Discernment is not a test where you pass or fail, or an interview where you hope to be good enough for the job.

When I think about discernment it reminds me of a woman I know who had a nice photograph of herself, her husband and three children. She bought a frame, took it to the framer and asked him to put it on the picture. 'No, lass, you don't want to do that!' he told her. Seeing that she was a bit put out, he disappeared into the back shop. After a few minutes he returned with a smaller, oval frame. Without a word, he placed the new frame on one section of the picture, around her two daughters' heads. Instantly, an ordinary family picture was transformed into a work of art: his reframing was able to draw out the core of the picture to reveal a beauty that had been hidden before. Only the discerning eye of the craftsman could see it.

In our discernment process we hope to look at the picture of your life and let the Holy Spirit highlight the core of the person God has made you and draw out the heart of your individual vocation. Then we want to find which 'frame', which outward form of service, best fits your life to bring out its beauty, fulfilment for you, service to God's kingdom and glory to God. ∎

Read

Francis Dewar, **Called or Collared? An Alternative Approach to Vocation** (London: SPCK, 2000)

Jonathan Lawson and Gordon Mundell, **Hearing the Call: Stories of Young Vocation** (London: SPCK, 2014)

Magdalen Smith, **Steel Angels** (London: SPCK, 2014)

Think

1. Recall a time when you believe God asked you to do something. How did you know it was God?

2. Who has helped you to see more clearly what God wants you to do, and how have they helped?

3. What is the benefit of discussing your possible future with other people?

Act

Visit the Tomorrow's Calling website at www.tomorrowscalling.org and read more about the process. Consider attending the next Vocations Conference.

AMONG THE MANY HOPES

Roddy Hamilton

Among the many hopes
and through the many dreams
may I discern
the one that fits with me:

that shape you made me,
that person you honed,
those experiences held,
those questions I ask.

Take these,
this distinctive combination
of my unique individuality
and vulnerable faith,
and find my space
shared with,
and given for
others in your body,
the Body of Christ.

May I desire less what I shall be,
and discern more of who I need to be
for your kingdom,
in community
with all your people,
and with faith still more uncertain than sure
may I dare step into the adventure,
apprehensive of where I might be going,
and trust the mix of grace and gift
with which you have created me,
and may I give thanks
for whatever will be
in your name
and for your purpose.

Amen

Responding to a Call

My Story: responding to God's call

Tommy MacNeil

I heard in a sermon a few years ago that 'nothing happens in God's kingdom and in the world without a declaration'. In creating the universe, God didn't just think creation into being: God spoke it into being: Genesis 1 tells us that 'And God said...' Similarly, when we speak out about a promise that God has placed in our heart, we begin to see it take shape; vision becomes reality.

Take our story here at Martin's Memorial Church in Stornoway. Our youth work had been flourishing, and despite expanding our premises, we had run out of room again. And so we made the courageous decision to build a new facility – despite having no ground, no money, and no plan. We did, however, have a vision, and the words in Isaiah 54.2 – 'Enlarge the place of your tent, stretch your tent curtains wide, do not hold back; lengthen your cords, strengthen your stakes'. Trusting in God and the vision placed on our hearts, we saw a developing story of God-incidences that made it clear that this vision, which was to become known as 'The Shed', was not just our idea: it was God's idea.

Six months later we owned the derelict building over the back wall of the church, together with its grounds and a generous donation – all gifted to us by its owner to provide for 'The Shed'. After two years of planning permissions, finance planning, employing local builders and demolishing the old building, we were on our way. And finally, three years after first speaking out the vision God had given us, we were welcoming Prince Edward and Countess Sophie to Stornoway to officially open the centre: a royal seal of approval in more ways than one!

And now? 'The Shed' has been open for over a year and is already working beyond capacity. We have two full-time employees and two new staff arriving on placement from the Job Centre to develop the work. A full youth and community programme means that it is open morning, noon, and night. And most importantly, we not only have a new building, but have moved from being 'a one-day-a-week service church to a seven-day-a-week serving church!' As Hudson Taylor once said: 'God's work done in God's way will never lack God's supply.'[1]

So let me ask you, what do you see? What vision do you have in your heart? What is the next part of God's vision for your church? I encourage you - no, I challenge you – even dare you to speak it out and to watch what happens when you do. There is power in what we speak!

[1] F. H. Taylor and G. Taylor, *Hudson Taylor and the China Inland Mission: The Growth of a Work of God* (Littleton, CO; Mississauga, ON; Kent, TN: OMF, 1995), p.42

CALL TO THE KINGDOM AND GOD'S MISSION

Sandy Forsyth

Practical Theology, Theology & Religious Studies,
University of Glasgow

If you are beleaguered by doubts about what it might mean to answer God's call, you may be asking yourself: 'What am I actually to do? What is the overall goal and how do I translate that into a particular form of action?' Maybe there could be reassurance and a sense of onward direction from several sources.

First of all, we answer the call from within the *missio Dei* (the mission of God). The focus of the Christian life is mission, which is the vital interaction, in word and deed, of God's love and purpose in salvation with the life of the world. However, it is *God's* mission, not ours. God's mission is not reliant on our human ingenuity alone, nor is the Church the sole object and agent of God's mission. We seek to play our part in God's loving purposes for all creation, but we take comfort that God is the directing force, and not us. Instead, we look to discern what God is doing, and then participate.

In that context, our sense of call is not necessarily hidebound to a fixed role for all time coming; instead our call is to availability for God, depending on God's purposes for us. In answering the call, by releasing ourselves to be compliant with the will of God, we are placing ourselves in God's hands, to be led and directed towards any post, any task, any role near or far; remembering always that God will provide us with the tools and the strength to prevail.

It is through our actions that we might begin to learn what God's purposes for us may be. Mission takes us beyond the Church and into the world, for a goal higher than the building up of an institution. The great Church of Scotland leader of the mid-twentieth century, Tom Allan, believed that the only way to prepare a church for mission was to do mission itself. It is in our attempts to be part of God's mission, by engaging with the world in Christ's name, that we begin to discover in earnest where, and to what, God is sending us.

Frederick Buechner described the location of where God will lead us in answer to the call as where our 'deep gladness' meets the 'deep hunger' of the world.[1] Identifying that place thus requires, first an immersion in the 'deep hunger' of the world, and, second while we are there, a process of prayerful discernment to find a 'deep gladness', the God-inspired passion that will lead us forward.

66 God-inspired
passion that
will lead us
forward.

No one doubts, however, that discernment can be a testing process, often marked as much by self-examination and 'failure' as much as by revelation and exhilaration. John Ortberg writes of discerning a calling that we must recognise that its terms may not be immediately explicit, nor might our gifts already be fully developed to meet the tasks ahead. Instead, God calls us with a warning that there is 'some assembly required'! For Ortberg, discerning a calling may therefore:

- push a human being to heights of self-exploration and judgement
- demand a ruthless assessment of our own gifts and shortcomings
- require some cherished dreams to be abandoned as a consequence.[2]

Answering a sense of call, and discerning its direction, is therefore an ongoing process of questing and development, with God changing our perspectives, enabling and empowering us to fulfil the goals, and opening and closing the doors to potential opportunities before us.

Fulfilling that calling in the context of God's mission in the world is, in the words of Richard Bauckham, a movement from 'the one to the many'.[3] It is, for Bauckham, a reflection of the repeated movement in Scripture from the 'particular to the universal', whose ultimate example lies in the movement from the person and history of Jesus Christ towards the flourishing of the kingdom of God, wherein God's purposes are fully achieved for the world.[4]

How then do we likewise move from ourselves and our sense of calling, 'the particular', towards building the kingdom of God, 'the universal'? Bauckham argues that the Biblical narrative shows us three movements of constant renewal and growth from God: what he calls 'temporal' movement into a new future; 'spatial' movement towards new horizons; and the 'people' movement of a new humanity.[5] In our actions in response to God's call, we are thus seeking to replicate those scriptural movements from the life and witness of Jesus towards the fulfilment of the kingdom – always seeking to engage with new futures, new horizons and new people.

In recent times four grand narratives have characterised the Church's thinking on how our mission is called to relate to the *missio Dei*:

- 'Proclamation' (1950s) – our mission is to evangelise the world through the church
- 'Shalom' (1960s) – our mission is to promote peace, integrity, community, harmony and justice
- 'Liberation' (1970s) – our mission is to engage in God-inspired action for the poor and marginalised
- 'Reconciliation' and 'dialogue' (1990s to date) – our mission is to demand open dialogue, humility and respect for the other, seeking the reconciliation of people in conflict, both to each other and to God.[6]

Whether in God's mission to the world we feel called to proclaim the Gospel in order to evangelise, or to promote community and peace, or to stand up for the poor and the outcast, or to seek to reconcile people in dialogue, we are moving towards the 'universal' of the kingdom. In the process we are discerning the relationship between our 'deep gladness' and the world's 'deep need', available and willing to answer God's call in our lives, whatever the outcome. ■

Read

John Ortberg, **If You Want to Walk on Water, You've Got to Get Out of the Boat**, (Grand Rapids, Michigan: Zondervan Publishing, 2001)

Richard Bauckham, **Bible and Mission: Christian Witness in a Postmodern World**, (Milton Keynes: Paternoster Press, 2003)

Stuart Murray, **Church after Christendom: Church and Mission in a Strange New World**, (Milton Keynes: Paternoster Press, 2004)

Think

1. What might answering a call to availability for the mission of God in the world mean in your life?

2. In what ways might you move from the 'one to the many' for God's kingdom?

3. Which of the 'grand narratives' of mission do you find most helpful?

Act

Read Matthew 14.25-32. What 'first step out of the boat' will you take, like Peter, and how will God support you?

[1] From *Wishful Thinking: A Theological ABC*, 1973, quoted in John Ortberg, *If You Want to Walk on Water, You've Got to Get Out of the Boat* (Grand Rapids, Michigan: Zondervan Publishing, 2001), pp.60–61

[2] Ortberg, *If You Want to Walk on Water*, p.59

[3] Richard Bauckham, *Bible and Mission: Christian Witness in a Postmodern World*, (Milton Keynes: Paternoster Press, 2003), pp.27-54

[4] **Bauckham**, *Bible and Mission*, pp.11 & 84

[5] **Bauckham**, *Bible and Mission*, pp.13-15

[6] For a helpful summary, see Stanley H. Skreslet, *Comprehending Mission: The Questions, Methods, Themes, Problems and Prospects of Missiology*, (Maryknoll, New York: Orbis Books, 2012), pp.31-34

The Sower
hearing and acting

Matthew 13

Alison Jack
New College, University of Edinburgh

The Parable of the Sower appears in the first three Gospels, each time one of the first parables to be heard from the mouth of Jesus. It is one of the few parables to which is added an explanation. The parable is told to the crowd and then, later, when Jesus is alone with his closest followers, he explains what it means. From the dynamics of the story there seems to be a suggestion that the more you are willing to hear, follow and obey, the more revelation you are offered. Hearing and acting on what you hear leads you closer to Jesus and to understanding what it means to share in the work of his kingdom.

On the face of things, the story is very simple. It is a description of what happens when seed is sown: the nature of the soil on which the seed lands affects the quality of the harvest. Without the explanation, the focus of the story could be the sower, or the seed, or the ground, or the harvest. We have probably all heard a sermon which takes one or other of these elements and runs with it. But the explanation which follows the parable suggests that either Jesus himself, or the editors of the Gospels, thought that the condition of the soil was the key element in the story. As such, the story works as a warning to the disciples of Jesus that their preaching of the gospel will not always succeed; the story also works in the context of the early Church, encouraging hearers to be like the good soil rather than the rocky or shallow or weed-choked terrain.

More complexities stem from the question of whether or not the sower was acting in a way which those involved in agriculture in Jesus' time would recognise, or whether he was sowing the seed in an outrageously wasteful and extravagant manner. Was it normal for three-quarters of the seed effectively to be lost? The debate as to whether the story tells of extravagance

or normality continues in respect of the extent of the harvest described. Was a ten-fold increase in the seed sown the expected yield, or a harvest of miraculous proportions? Put simply, is this a story from the realm of fairy tale and hyperbole, or is it a straightforward tale bristling with realism? Over the centuries the balance of scholarly opinion has shifted and changed, but, generally speaking, today the harvest is viewed as generous but not spectacular, and the sowing technique is not outside the bounds of reason, as far as anyone can tell from this distance of time.

A harvest comes only when the hearing is accompanied by wholehearted action

Why should this matter to a reader who seeks to understand what the story means for them today, as they contemplate answering a call of some kind? That the parable is situated in the everyday world of work suggests that its message is not about waiting for miraculous signs. And it is not about demanding grand gestures from those who hear a whisper directed at them which has the ring of truth about it. Rather, it is about taking the first decisive step and acting in faithful response to the call from the context in which you find yourself. In the story, some of the seed sprouts, the message is heard and even causes joy in the lives of the hearers, but there is a shallowness to the response and the plants wither. A harvest comes only when the hearing is accompanied by wholehearted action, a response which wells up from the depths of the hearer, and which is productive of real change.

There are similarities here with the Parable of the Two Sons (Matthew 21.28–32). The one son says he will go and work in his father's vineyard, but in fact does nothing. The other son says he will not go and work for his father, but later changes his mind and goes. Jesus asks which son does the will of his father, and the answer is clear. Actions, in response to hearing the call, speak louder than fine words and good intentions. ∎

Read

Alyce M. McKenzie, **The Parables for Today** (Louisville: WJK Press, 2007)

Klyne Snodgrass, **Stories with Intent: A Comprehensive Guide to the Parables of Jesus** (Grand Rapids, MI: Eerdmans, 2008)

David Buttrick, **Speaking Parables: A Homiletic Guide** (Louisville: WJK Press, 2000), pp.64–70

Think

1. Play with the Parable of the Sower in your imagination: what do the seeds represent for you, and are there times when your response to the Gospel has been shallow, or negative, or fruitful?

2. Would it make any difference whether this parable were thought to be more like a fairy tale than a story marked by its realism?

3. The weeds that choke the seedlings are a potent image in our age which is often marked by information overload and stress. What weeds may there be in your life/church which prevent the Gospel being as fruitful as it might be?

Act

Pray that you might have ears to hear what God is saying to you in this story.

MINISTRY IN THE CHURCH OF SCOTLAND

Martin Johnstone
Council Secretary of Church & Society Council, Church of Scotland

John took me for a walk round part of Castlemilk. He was, at that point, one of two parish ministers serving this large post-war housing scheme on the south side of Glasgow. If the encounter went well, it was hoped that I would spend my time as an assistant minister in Castlemilk. It was wet. It was miserable. It was grey. It was hardly an auspicious start. And yet almost thirty years on, that afternoon remains indelibly printed in my memory. In the course of a two-hour walk, we must have stopped and spoken in depth to at least fifteen people, while at least three times that number hailed us from buses, from tenement blocks, even high-rise flats, and from the other side of the road. 'Hello there, Mr Miller!' People shared their deepest pain and struggle alongside their regular stream of good news and celebration. I left drenched and exhilarated.

Although I had grown up in the Church, it was my first real insight into the glory of parish (or territorial) ministry – a ministry which gives us the extraordinary privilege of being alongside people from every part of a community. It is a model of ministry which has changed out of all recognition over the centuries and is continuing to change at a remarkable pace. However, the Church of Scotland remains committed to this model of ministry in every part of Scotland. In the past it was a core building-block for universal education and healthcare. In the present, it equips people to worship, to pray and to participate in thousands of small, faith-inspired acts of kindness and generosity as well as enabling incredible youth work and inspiring care for many of Scotland's most disadvantaged citizens. If parish ministry is our calling, there is no more glorious, exhilarating and exciting a place in which to be.

Although I had felt a call to the ministry of Word and Sacrament at a relatively early age, I had spent many of my adolescent years desperately trying to run away from it. That afternoon in Castlemilk helped to restore my deep sense that this was indeed what God was asking of me. Subsequently, I had the incredible honour of spending ten years in parish ministry in Bellshill (Lanarkshire).

One of the nicest things that anyone has ever said to me was when I was leaving Bellshill. In presenting me with a silver quaich on behalf of the school where I had been chaplain, the Head Teacher said that I hadn't just been a good friend to the school but I had been the school's best friend. Laying aside the sort of hyperbole that happens at such times, and being really clear that I was certainly no better and probably a whole lot worse than many of my peers, it is an indication of the sort of awesome position that a parish minister continues to occupy in today's Scotland.

> " **Parish ministry means that we have a commitment to the whole community rather than just to those who turn up on a Sunday.**

If school chaplaincy is one of the key elements of parish ministry, so too is the opportunity to get involved in some of the many activities within the local community and the great variety of organisations and agencies, bearing in mind that it is not possible to commit to everything.

There is no longer an automatic right to be involved but my experience has always been that folks are delighted to see the local minister and to have her or him as a core part of what is going on. Pastorally, in ten years I was never once refused entry to a house, albeit I was once confused with the window cleaner!

Parish ministry means that we have a commitment to the whole community rather than just to those who turn up on a Sunday. People sometimes complain that this means that some just make use of the Church or the services of a minister. That has never been my experience. Rather, in every funeral, wedding or pastoral visit, I have encountered people with a wistfulness for the Gospel who frequently teach me about faith, rather than the other way around.

Although parish ministry is about being there for everyone within the neighbourhood, there is clearly that incredibly special relationship with the church community. The commitment to nurture faith and discipleship is at the absolute heart of the calling of a Church of Scotland minister. There is no use denying that sometimes it feels like there is a bit of a tension between parish ministry and congregational ministry. However, for me at least, it was a rich and exhilarating tension. The task of praying with people deepened my prayer life. The responsibility of leading worship caused me to grapple with the tough issues of faith. And above all, the privilege of encouraging others to find and develop their God-given gifts helped me to grow into a deeper understanding of the ministry of all God's people and to see my own ministry within that context. ■

Read

Raymond Fung, **The Isaiah Vision** (Eugene, Oregon: Wipf & Stock, 2009)

Alan Billings, **Making God Possible – the Task of Ordained Ministry Present and Future** (London: SPCK, 2010)

Think

1. What would Scotland look like without a Christian community in every neighbourhood?

2. What do you think the shape of ministry in the Church of Scotland will look like in ten years' time?

3. What part can you play in the ministry of all God's people in your local church and community?

Act

Write a prayer of thanksgiving for the church's parish ministry and then use that prayer in your personal devotions every day for a month.

CALLING TO NEW WAYS

Shirley Grieve
Go For It Fund Manager, Ministries Council

The Church is funding new ways of ministry. Since 2012 the Church's *Go For It Fund* has helped to fund, train and support new forms of Christian community. The Church commits over £1 million every year to fund these projects: this is a loud statement that the Church recognises that God is calling people to pioneer new ways. Go For It funding has enabled many people to step out into the call God has placed in their heart to see the kingdom come here on earth. God calls us all to love and serve the world: what does this look like in your life?

Our experience in *Go For It* is that God is calling many different people in many different ways for many different ministries, but with the one purpose of sharing the hope of the gospel with people in local communities. Responding to call is not easy, and for some it demands that they give up some of the most precious commodities we have: time and money. But time and again we see brave individuals responding to God's prompting to go and serve local communities with the promise of the Gospel.

We are often asked 'What is a typical *Go For It* project?' There is no one 'type', the breadth of work is enormous, but leadership, ministry, service, vocation, call, are common characteristics of the work that is taking place.

The Fund has five key criteria:
- Meeting identified needs in the community
- Nurturing Christian faith within and beyond the Church
- Tackling poverty and social injustice
- Developing new ecclesial Christian communities
- Creating work that is innovative and shares good practice.

Projects anchor their work across two or more of these criteria. Some are very deliberately setting out to develop pioneering new church communities within the Church of Scotland. Others are

intent on tackling issues within our society that lead to the marginalisation of people and whole communities. Most projects see these two objectives as one: that as we build new ecclesial communities we can together be part of building solutions for injustice.

The *Gateways* project is a great example of a project developing a new ecclesial community, and Jill's story shows how new communities are helping people to discover more of God and more of themselves. Along with her husband and two children, Jill was encouraged to be part of the team that developed the Gateways Gathering, and since then she has become a member of the Core Team and her husband is one of the trustees. Here Jill tells the impact this missional project made to her:

> *I was periodically attending the local Church of Scotland which I really enjoyed going to, but with two small children and no room for a crèche it was becoming more difficult. We were then introduced to Gateways. This has really been a Godsend to us. We went to the first Gateways Gathering and have not looked back since. I continue to go to our local church sometimes, but have struggled recently as my father had been diagnosed with prostate cancer earlier this year and I struggled in the formal setting and cried every time the hymns were being sung! The Gateways team have been amazing. I have been able to continue my worship in a more relaxed setting. We have made friends at Gateways and spend time with them outside of the Gateways setting, which is lovely.*

> *Gateways has helped me maintain my faith, spend time with my family and allow my children to learn about God in a relaxing fun way. I have also made new friends and enjoyed many social activities. The support is always there for you but is never forced on you, which is what I am comfortable with.*

The Church, through projects like *Go For It*, is seeking new ways to connect with those outside of the Church. The Fund is enabling the Church to become part of transformational conversations with parishes and communities throughout Scotland. We are currently funding over 120 projects across 34 Presbyteries that employ over 180 staff, utilise the skills of around 1,600 volunteers and reach out to over 25,000 beneficiaries. Imagine what this means for the work of mission around this country! And imagine what God has in store as we respond to the different new ventures to which God is calling us.

Kate's Kitchen responded to the call. They sensed the need to set up a warm place, a haven where those suffering on the outside of society could come and feel safe and accepted. This people-centred ministry relies on the role of volunteers; people who are inspired to be pastors and apostles in their community.

... imagine what God has in store as we respond to the different new ventures to which God is calling us.

An 18 year old young man came to the Kitchen with his girlfriend. For the first two weeks he sat with her and only spoke to the support worker who moved round the room speaking to those who were there. At the end of the third week he came and asked if he could have a food parcel which he got, but as a result of the discussion that followed, a raft of issues was highlighted.

He was homeless, he had very little in the way of personal possessions and badly needed new boots as his current footwear leaked, he was unemployed but also sanctioned for not turning up at a meeting and not doing enough job searching. The priority was to get him shelter, so an appointment was made with the homeless officer to start resolving the housing issue. A meeting was set for the young man and the support worker to begin to look at employment and education possibilities. The first step was to try to firm up a routine for him to do job searches so that he would not be sanctioned again in the short term and then to work towards longer-term solutions.

The difference this made to the young man was fairly dramatic. He had dry feet on a wet day, he could go out with clean clothes on, he had his own supported house to go back to at night and he has not been sanctioned since. This means he does not go deeper into debt just to survive and he can plan how he spends his money.

The Church is nurturing potential apostles, prophets, evangelists, pastors and teachers that are needed to see God's kingdom here on earth. These projects are places that are reaching out in new ways and are like incubators of faith. These are the communities where new shoots are coming through and they are best placed to nurture people's sense of call.

Flemington Hallside Youth Project received funding to reach out to young people through detached youth work as well as through providing clubs and activities. We can worry about falling numbers in churches, about fewer people coming forward for ministry and wonder how people can discern a call, but work such as that which is taking place at Flemington Hallside is offering real opportunities for both a call to service and helping a call to ministry to be heard. If young people don't even know that the role of

ministry exists and what it might entail, they are much further away from even being able to begin to discern how God may be leading them. The story of John, a 16 year-old young man who attends the project, helps us to understand more about the nature of call:

Prior to the appointment of our youth worker John had made the decision to stop coming to church as he had been finding it boring and irrelevant to his life. After our youth worker came into post, John's Mum encouraged him to come along to Church again. He initially attended 'Ignite' a group for primary 7 to secondary 4 on a Sunday morning. He quickly settled into the group and soon started asking faith based questions and was keen to learn more. A few months into the project we launched a group for young people secondary 4 to 6 and John has been fully committed to attending this group ever since. He frequently talks of his enjoyment in being back at church and has said that without the youth project he wouldn't have returned.

By turning up at all events organised by the project, we see his commitment; his volunteering to be a leader shows how his faith has developed over the year, enabling him to share this with others. John's Mum regularly tells us about how happy she is with the change in John's faith, 'John has come on in leaps and bounds since joining. Without your input and support he would never have been able to do some of the things that the youth project has allowed him to do: take part in team work, camp and explore his faith'.

John talks of his enjoyment of being in church. He has told us he is keen to learn things about Jesus and faith, and he continues to ask deeper faith questions. He now helps in the wider Church, with AV projection on Sunday morning, welcome duty and carrying the Bible – this is important in giving a visible sign to all the congregation of the centrality of young people in our Church's life.

Throughout these stories we see God's love in action through people who have responded to the calling that God has placed upon their lives. The stories are all different but have the same faithful God at the heart: how will you respond to God's call? ■

Read

Michael Frost and Alan Hirsch, **The Shaping of Things to Come: Innovation and Mission For The 21st-Century Church** (Michigan, Baker Press, 2013)

The Poverty Truth Commission Report, 2014-2016 (Faith in Community Scotland, 2016)

Mark Butcher, **Create! A toolkit for creative problem solving in the not-for-profit sector** (London, Directory of Social Change, 2005)

Find more resources on:
www.churchofscotland.org.uk/serve/go_for_it

Think

1. How can you link your own life in your congregation or community to our Lord's call to leave everything and follow him?

2. Are you being called to work alongside and with the people in your community to find solutions to local need?

3. Who are the apostles, prophets, evangelists, pastors and teachers in your community – can you spot them already or do you need to nurture them?

Act

Take time to journal about *who* God is calling you to: begin to imagine what God might have in store.

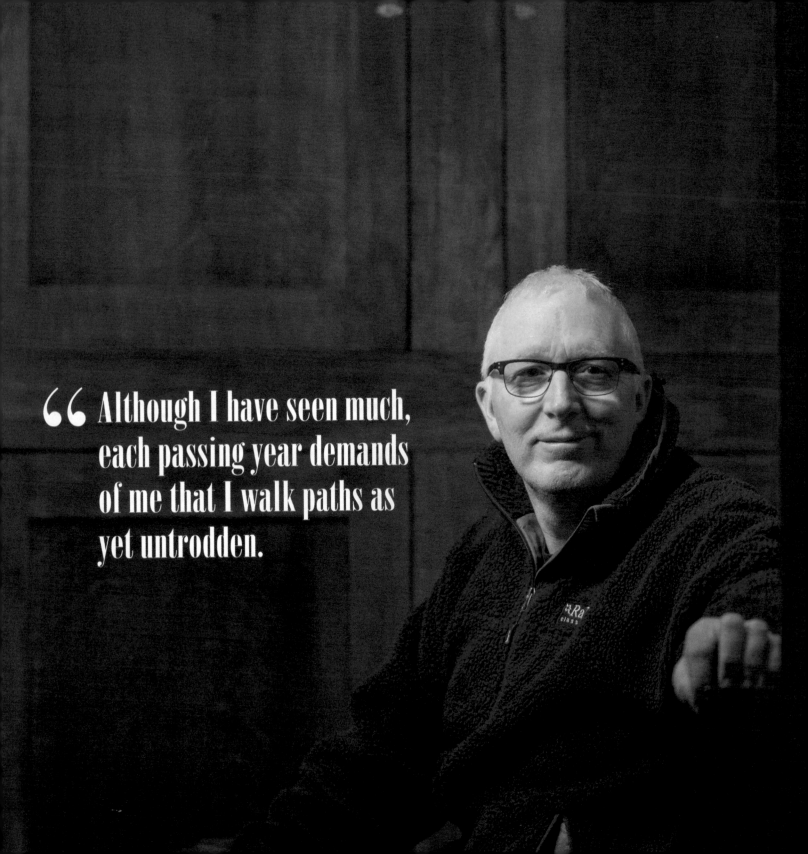

66 Although I have seen much,
each passing year demands
of me that I walk paths as
yet untrodden.

THE TRODDEN ROAD

Martin Fair

Minister of Arbroath, St. Andrew's

'Anywhere, apart from the east coast of Scotland.' That was the deal I struck when answering God's call to ministry. Born and bred in Glasgow, I had no intention of 'emigrating' to the other side of the country ...

So what am I doing in Arbroath? It does not get much more 'east coast' than Arbroath!

The first thing I had to learn about responding to God's calling was that it was not for me to set conditions upon it. You either say 'yes' to God or 'no'. To respond with 'Yes, but' is not really an obedient response at all. The would-be prophet, Isaiah, responds to God's call with 'I will go! Send me!' (Isaiah 6.8). No sign there of any geographical or circumstantial limits upon his 'yes'. And the story of Jonah should further serve as a warning about placing restrictions on the 'where' and 'to whom' of God's call to serve. (Jonah 1.1–3) He discovered the hard way that there is no 'getting away from the Lord'.

And, of course, when we learn to trust God absolutely, and to say 'yes' without condition, we discover that God knew best all along! Looking at a list of vacant charges back in the autumn of 1991, I would not even have considered St. Andrew's, Arbroath as an option and yet my 24 years in that church have been positive and happy, and there has been a profound sense of God's blessing and provision and guidance. It was absolutely the right place for me. I would not change places with anyone.

Of course, it has not all been plain sailing. Nothing of value comes easily. I cannot even begin to quantify how hard I have worked through these years, and there are some scars to testify to the fact that at times ministry is extremely tough.

On my very first Sunday, an elder of what had just become my first charge came to the vestry to wish me well, just a few moments before the start of the service. He reached out to shake my hand and in that very moment suffered a massive heart attack and died on the spot – in my vestry at five-to-eleven. What a start to my ministry! I still have no idea how I came through that first service but I do remember telling myself that, having survived that, there would be nothing in the future that could overwhelm me.

I was right, but only just. By the end of that first month in Arbroath, I had had to stand at the bedside of one of the congregation's best-loved young women and, with her family, watch her die. I will never forget conducting her funeral service with her five-year-old son and seven-year-old daughter sitting right in front of me. I had never felt so inadequate and so useless in all of my life.

Within days of that, the local funeral director called me again, this time to tell me that a man in his early forties had taken his own life and had been found, by his teenage daughter, hanging in the garage. I will never forget going to visit that family. I was only 27, with very little of what is dubbed 'life experience', and I was fast learning that my Bachelor of Divinity degree alone was not going to be enough for all that I was going to face.

At that point, you had better be sure of your 'call'. Standing in front of broken, shattered people, you have got nothing else to stand on other than your absolute sense that 'God called me to be the minister in this place.' As I discovered in these early months and years, when you have got nothing else to offer, knowing God's call upon your life is enough – more than enough.

I have travelled far since those early experiences; I am well down that well-trodden path. Even so, there is still no greater privilege than to sit with one of 'my people' through those critical life moments. There is still no better thrill – and no more daunting responsibility – than to stand before 'my people' on a Sunday morning with the challenge of bringing to them something from the eternal Word of God. And there is still little to match the deep-down joy of seeing one of 'my people' discovering faith in Christ or offering themself in God's service. Twice, young people have come to me asking to be baptised – in the sea! Those who know the waters at Arbroath will know well that they have an 'arctic' quality to them, and yet those occasions are right at the top of my 'most fulfilling' list.

Although I have seen much, each passing year demands of me that I walk paths as yet untrodden. And that is what keeps it fresh and exciting. New challenges to face up to. New people to share Good News with or to welcome into the family of Christ. New ways for us as a congregation to discover just how God wants us to express love in action.

There is never a day in ministry that does not require of those of us who have responded to God's call that we step out in faith – all over again.

Earlier, I wrote that 'I would not change places with anyone.' When you have ministered in the same place for so long, there is an attachment between you and 'your people' that is as strong as any familial bond you are likely to experience. Even so, just as I was obedient in responding to God's call to come to Arbroath, I must remain open to the possibility of God calling me elsewhere in the time that lies ahead.

There is only one question that really matters: 'Lord, how and where would you have me serve you?' ∎

Read

Ron Ferguson, **The Life of Geoffrey M. Shaw** (Gartocharn: Famedram Publishers, 1979)

John Stott, **I Believe in Preaching** (London: Hodder & Stoughton, 1982)

Leonard Sweet, **Summoned to Lead** (Grand Rapids, Michigan: Zondervan, 2004)

Think

1. Jonah was hugely reluctant to go to Nineveh (Jonah 1.1–3.) Why? What was he afraid of?

2. Might it be that you are setting limitations on your availability – saying to God, 'Yes, but ...'?

3. While some are called to travel abroad, and others are called to 'emigrate to the east coast of Scotland', consider the ways in which God might be calling you to minister right where you are.

Act

If you have even an inkling of an idea that God might be calling you, commit to speaking to someone about it by the end of this week.

TOMORROW'S
CALLING

tomorrowscalling.org

LOVE THAT FOREVER CALLS YOUR NAME

Roddy Hamilton

May you trust the paths that unfold for you,
may you wonder at the possibilities you find,
may you nurture the love that forever calls your name,
and holds you in the dream God has for you.

May you hear the call to be the gift you are,
and find the ministry only your being fits,
may you be guided by compassion for the other,
and dare to be generous in the love of God.

May you find inspiration through life in the Spirit
shaping from birth who God created you to be,
and travelling the journey you share with others,
in the ministry of giving, find the person you are.

May you know the Word restless in your soul,
may you be challenged to ask, seek and knock,
and in questioning the future may the door be opened
to discerning the call of the Lord Jesus Christ.

Amen

CALLED TO WHAT?
recovering a call for today

Martin Scott
Secretary to Council of Assembly

'It used to be so much simpler to test the *call*,' one of our Ministry Assessors remarked recently. Like so many areas of modern life, the shape and focus of ministry in the Church of Scotland is increasingly in flux. There is a sense in which that Assessor was right. When ministry was a clearly defined territorial task to a settled congregation in the context of a society which thought of itself as Christian and the national Church was something to which everyone somehow belonged (the 'Christendom' model), it was simpler to visualise the kind of person who would fit the role of Parish Minister. The task of assessment was never 'easy', but the stereotype of the 'ideal minister' may have been easier to visualise.

That is no longer the case, because we live in a post-Christian and post-Christendom society. In the past the Church occupied a place of privilege. The national Church in particular had a central place in civic life and the role of the Parish Minister was primarily to be a pastor and teacher to a settled congregation in a wider parish and community which recognised and acknowledged that role. Nowadays, however, the Church is increasingly moving to the margins of society, seeking to make its voice heard where there is a multiplicity of faiths and none. While there remains a significant degree of sympathy for the Church and its work throughout the country, fewer than 5% of people in Scotland connect regularly with its services. There is an increasing pressure from some quarters for any residue of Christian influence in civic society to be removed. In many ways, the Church today is nearer to its early roots than it has been for many centuries: we have to *earn* attention for the message to which we witness rather than *assume* interest. In this context, discerning a call to ministry has become more complex, and it rightly gives rise to a fundamental question: called to *what*?

The question is intensified by the outlook of many of the congregations to which Parish Ministers are called. Their expectation is still largely for a 'pastor-teacher' who will offer care for the parish (and especially for the members) and will preach/teach the Word. There may well be other aspirations – most commonly that the minister should bring in new people, especially *young* people, but the lingering hope even if that happens, is that this will revive and restore the old, settled ways. The minister is thus often expected to be both a guardian of a received model of ministry and at the same time an innovator: it is frequently a recipe for conflict and stress.

A number of our contributors in this guide have pointed us to biblical stories where people have experienced the call of God to service. They remind us of the various ways in which people have responded to Christ's call – so the question, 'Called to what?', is

The time is ripe for us to rediscover the missing roles - the calling of God to some to be Apostles, some Prophets and some Evangelists.

an important one for us to consider, even if the answer is not as easy as it might once have appeared. A good starting place is surely Ephesians 4.1-16, where the writer is urging readers to strive for unity in the body of Christ. Verses 11-12 read: 'The gifts he gave were that some would be apostles, some prophets, some evangelists, some pastors and teachers, to equip the saints for the work of ministry, for building up the body of Christ.'

The first thing that Ephesians 4 tells us about ministry is that it belongs to 'the saints' – by which is meant *all* of God's people. The purpose of all five roles in verse 11 (apostles; prophets; evangelists; pastors; teachers) is to *equip the saints.* It is not that any individual should become omni-competent, but that all should be enabled to use the gifts they have been given in the ministry of the *whole body.* There is an underlying implication, however, that those called to the 'equipping' function will exercise a degree of leadership in ensuring that the gifts of others are nurtured. The writer is clearly experienced enough in dealing with those who are called to exercise leadership to know that there is the potential for *disunity* – hence the emphasis of the whole passage on the theme of unity within the diversity of gifts in the one body of Jesus Christ.

As we already noted, ministry in the Church of Scotland has overwhelmingly focused on two of these five roles – the pastor and teacher – combined in one person. Of all the roles, these are the ones which least obviously demand leadership qualities, to the extent that many who felt called to minister in the 'settled' model will say that they were not called to leadership. By contrast, however, *apostles* in the early Church were seen as those who pioneered the work, the strategic thinkers who sought to establish new communities of faith. In a Christendom setting, where the Church could assume that everyone was born to some degree within its power, apostles could be viewed as something belonging to the past – no longer necessary.

That is certainly not our context today. The *prophets* were always the awkward squad, edgy folk whose ideological outlook challenges our structures and thinking. In a Christendom context they were particularly unwelcome as disturbing the 'peace' and the established order. Our setting today cries out for some to take on this role. The

evangelists knew the skills of communicating the faith to others and wooing them by word and witness. In a Christendom Church they hardly seemed necessary when people's participation could be assumed, or even at its worst, compelled. The national Church today can make no such assumptions.

Attendance in the Church of Scotland has been steadily falling over many years and the age profile of our current ministry (almost 85% of ministers are over 50) is at a critical level. We know that the 'settled' model of ministry simply cannot continue to fulfil the remit of a 'national Church', given the projected fall in ministerial numbers from 850 to around 600 by the early 2020s. This could seem like just cause for despair and a sense of hopelessness, a recipe for exhaustion and poor morale among our ministers. Yet it need not be so. The time is ripe for us to rediscover the missing roles[1] - the calling of God to some to be Apostles, some Prophets and some Evangelists. This is not to leave behind some pastors and some teachers, but to return their calling to a proper perspective within the broader leadership whose task it is to equip 'all the saints' for the ministry of the one body of Jesus Christ.

If all the saints are to be effective in ministry, they will need the leadership and support of those to whom a specific calling to equip is given. The Church of Scotland has been affirming for more than 20 years the need for a team-based approach to ministry, and this requires both people who are willing to work in teams and those who will take on a leadership role. Not all leaders look or act the same – there are varied gifts of leadership and the five-fold model of Ephesians 4 provides a pointer to some of the key types. That three of these have for generations too often been ignored in our understanding of 'call' to ministry in the Church of Scotland leaves a significant gap in our resourcing for the mission and ministry of Jesus Christ. It can hardly surprise us, then, that our 'saints' so often feel ill-equipped.

Called to what? The wisdom of the writer to the Ephesians is that all the saints are called to ministry, but that within that wider calling there lies a vocation to a variety of leadership focused on the equipping of others – apostles; prophets; evangelists; pastors; teachers. It is a more expansive and inspirational vision of ministry than that to which we have become accustomed. In its recovery may well lie the seeds of the reinvigoration of Christian life and community together for which so many of us within the Church look and for which the parish communities to which we belong are waiting.

Is God calling you to be part of this vision? ∎

[1] See in particular, A. Hirsch and T. Catchin, *The Permanent Revolution: Apostolic Imagination and Practice for the 21st Century Church* (San Fransisco: Jossey-Bass, 2012).

SAINT ANDREW PRESS

Learn - Exploring Faith

This welcoming resource for new communicants can be run by your local church as a short and inspiring course.
Echoing the Profession of Faith as found in the Book of Common Order, it is also ideal for individuals who want to privately begin to explore what the Christian faith means.

ISBN 978-0-86153-928-4

People of the Way

Based on the Church of Scotland's Heart & Soul theme for the whole Church for the whole year, these fresh, beautifully crafted prayers, meditations, blessings and prayer activities help you to deepen your relationship with God, allowing time to think and space to listen.They prompt action and movement when the words just don't seem enough.

ISBN 978-0-86153-992-5

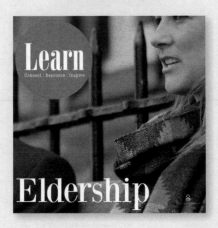

Learn - Eldership

Sold over 8,000 copies! Nominated for publishing award!
This popular publication is based on the affirmation that every elder takes.
This invaluable resource provides new and existing elders with a diverse range of articles by leading figures in the Church of Scotland.

ISBN 978-0-86153-924-6

www.churchofscotland.org.uk/learn

standrewpress.hymnsam.co.uk

TAKE A PEW

tomorrowscalling.org

Join this vital conversation about the Church of Scotland.